MW01279992

Queen Cadeena the Quintessence:

The MANyoUSCRIPT

Christina D Parker

Written, Edited, and Illustrated by Christina D Parker

Published and printed in the United States

1st Edition Printed and Published by Kindle/Amazon Publishing, Independently Published

ISBN 979-8-747-40930-9

Dedication

I believe in giving honor where it is due, so this book is dedicated to one person only. I've written so many dedications over the years in books that I've aspired to publish, but never did due to procrastination, self-doubt, fear of success, vulnerability, and exposure among other things. I'd use the purposed excuse of engulfing myself in other projects and needs of others, and sometimes it was just life itself. Nevertheless, time kept moving, but wasn't moving me closer to an actual date or progress toward my dream of being a published author and poet. It wasn't until I reached an extremely low point last year, one of the lowest in my life, that an unusual person from my past unexpectedly re-emerged 21 years after our last encounter, and changed my life (saved my life, literally), that I became inspired and motivated enough to see this project through to the end. Unbeknownst to either of us, our reunion would begin the journey of a lifetime. We reunited in person in the fall of 2020. Once we figured out the gift and talent of writing we commonly shared, it was decided on Nov. 20th that we'd release our first published works together six months to that day on May 20, 2021. It was as if we automatically knew we would still be significantly in each other's lives, and low and behold, we made it! So, I included 21 of the countless poems I've written over the years (in this first of many works to come) to signify the 21 years we spent apart. I am proud to write on this day, that I dedicate this book to the one I can now officially call, Author Lenton A. Ferguson aka *Poo*, more affectionately, *my PooBonny*! Thank you for believing in me, standing with me, walking with me, and being mentally strong enough to break through my barriers and fight wars on my behalf in order to save me from myself and the ones I lost pieces of myself to while trying at this thing called life and love-- all while waging your own personal battles. We're living proof that if you put out good things, good things will come back to you. Here's to forgotten seeds planted that have taken root and will continually bring us plentiful harvest for years to come! Oh, and congratulations on your first of many published works! Good job, Hammer! We did it!!! I love you for life for loving me back to life!!! #SelfMade

Queen Cadeena, the Quintessence:
THE MAN*yo*USCRIPT

Poetic Interludes: Flirting

What would it take to make you mine;

ageing like a vineyard wine

always so fine even better with time-

you are working that grown and sexy

Whatcha doin later, call me- text me,

tell me I'm your one and only plan

the reason you're no longer a lonely man

3/15/16

1

Extra: defined

What I have to offer
Is greater than the usual amount or
number of ways it's been given
Especially when it's not hidden
You see, my love
Provides so much more that it's
Supplementary
Not rocket science, yet so elementary
It furthers one's own emotions like an auxiliary
See my heart beats for you
Your heart's rhythm is ancillary to mine
In step keeping time with
The verse and rhyme
I am to you a subsidiary, your partner in crime
Never coming secondary unless by way of an
Added bonus
To a greater extent than usual
I am exceptionally aesthetically pleasing
Particularly very unusually and extremely lovable
Cute, cuddly, ever so huggable

Additionally, I can be a little too crazy
Extraordinarily overzealous and extremely jealous
But that's just because of how uncommonly
remarkably my loyalty is
Still I'll outstandingly amazingly charm you until
all you see is the sparkle in my eyes
Conspicuously and never disguised
I really, awfully, terribly, seriously
Love you with all I have
And seriously mucho majorly aim to please
So whenever you have the pleasure of the
addition of you plus me
Make sure you're ready to accept the addendum
Don't ever treat me like a walk-on
Besides that, don't even bother unless you can
accept that this Petra
Has a personality that is supernumerary-ly
EXTRA!!!

4/5/18

Poetry Junkie

I get high on words
Supply all the write words
Writ words- spoken I spit
Sight words
verbs, adjectives, in preposition
therefore to leave in retrospect
insight
I breathe in rhyme and
chime out rhythm
allegory and euphemism
to tell my stories and put you in 'em
Stanza after lined poetic verse
Floetic lyrics unrehearsed
Rapped, sang, orally dispersed
of the life and times
beats and rhymes
y'all go make me lose my mind up in here
Dem words get to ringing in my ears
penetrating my psyche
a little scared but like Nike
I just do it
Ain't nothing to it when the pen hits the paper
I smoke the pad until I smell the vapor
of THC: Thoughts Highest Concentration
Elevated to the point that I found that
deferred dream
and translate the chirps that the caged bird sings

Desolate and lone on the lake with Frost
biting the coldness of dying when love is lost
in the world of Shakespeare
Though always relevant, he don't fit in here
cause the rhetoric in this generation
provokes sensationalism
My truth *is* my story
My rhyme *is* my glory
Long winded or short Haiku
I, too, feel the fear of ink drying
in the midst of verbal crying
So excuse me while I kiss the sky
and get higher with every hit
It don't take much to get lit
Words written and read are like fire
but to hear them spoken is like uncontrollable desire
I be feinin' for new words to take me higher
Thesaurus flunky, dictionary monkey-
open mic funky
beyond the margins of addiction
I'm a poetry junkie

6/21/16

Light-Skinned

I'm not street smart
cause I didn't grow up in it
but I have no shame in being an academic
that just makes us two sides of the same epidemic
I'm the little Brown girl who thought reading was cool
but not fundamental enough to keep me in school
cause beyond the playground life taught me new rules
I was too light to fit in, often ridiculed
by others' darkness within, however miniscule
they were in their thinking
The world around me closing in
originality shrinking
still, I strived to remain me
Growing up in the land of the free
where people freely give pompous opinions
to which the fuck I don't give
cause just like the next man I'm just trying to live
Standing tall on my soap box to vent
about how life should've, could've, would've went
if only I were a little different
If only I had that natural rhythm to dance on beat
had a fully proportioned ass to balance my feet
spoke broken English, Ebonics and slang
instead of ending my words with a valley girl twang

If I knew the value of a label maybe I'd wear one
If there were value to a name then you'd overstand, son
that my worth is the light ray beaming sun
to which I am the earth and all it encompasses
revealing fake ones in all their incompetence
I may not recognize the voice on a hip hop track
but that doesn't make me any more or less Black
I may not be consumed with the constant fight
of how it feels on the other side of White
I can't be down for the cause because I have White friends
I must not know better because I'm light-skinned
So I'll just use this White man's degree I earned
and apply it to these life lessons I've learned;
that Black is not a hue, but a state of mind
that the streets throw around when they can't find
a way out of the noose of mental chains
that you're not increasing intellect by getting brain
not building wealth with custom spinning chrome
or moving poor man's dreams into million dollar homes
You ain't going nowhere cause your boy made it out the hood
waiting to get put on off stolen goods
still awaiting the approval of the white hoods-
the same ones who profile us in our hoodies
threatened by a pocket full of goodies
Sad how it's them who know our truest potential
and how the repercussions would be exponential
If we discovered it within ourselves
But who am I to delve
into all this Black stuff
the girl who traded her perm for a puff

her weave for extensions of ancestral pride
outward cultural symbols for being real inside
So excuse me for having the privilege of avoiding the streets
cause my mama had a method of making ends meet
met the struggle with style and grace
hiding the pain with the smile on her face
Well now it's finally genuine
cause her little Brown girl has grown tough skin
no longer forced to hide within
Loud and boisterous the twang in my tongue
off beat on step cause I pound my own drum
I've been in the same place you came from
but don't want to be where you're going
cause the real Black pride is more than just knowing
following, tweeting, and reciting
lyrics and quotes that sound inciting
when you can't apply for a Black card
When you always standing guard
afraid of what rights you still have left to lose
Can't pay no bills but kill for new shoes
Nigga moments go down if you make the wrong moves
but starting a movement whenever the cops shoot-
Of course Black lives matter, but really what for
cause until you cross the threshold of oppression's door
to seize the purpose of our creator's plan
to be a self-guided, self-disciplined, self-made man
Then you'll always criticize your own as being traitors
see those with Agape love as haters
and stay in your comfortable box living off the man
staring at a programmed box living out his plan

8

to keep you dumbed down thinking you don't wanna be like them
when they're reaping the benefits of Kem-etic knowledge
and other sciences and technologies taught in college
that we pay for when it once came free
Free thought and wisdom flows naturally
from the undying root of our ancestry
that in any shade of melanin qualifies us to be
Greater than *he*
Equal at least, but more than less
kings and queens at best
but I digress and said all this to say
that in our differences we're one in same
So forgive me for the street knowledge I lack
for being born light-skinned, yet unapologetically
Black

7/1/16

Eyes of the Beholder

They looked upon me in innocence and respect
and formed an opinion that in retrospect was only part of
the truth
As they look upon me now I can see traces of our youth
Memories of a time when our chemistry was sublime, but
too many other things occupied our minds and yet somehow
it seems he was always there on time
Those eyes have seen so much, as so mine eyes have
seen the glory
of all the ugly-beautiful parts of life that became chapters in
our story
They hold the mystery of a sordid history of love gone
wrong, sad love songs and pieces of self lost that we never
recovered
Still somehow now discovering those missing pieces within
the reacquaintance of one another
Not only does that stare behold the object of his affection,
but it etched a deep intimate reflection of who I used to be
Sent me on a long awaited journey on finding my way back
to me
The way they found a way back to behold and reveal
secrets untold about how I've always held a fond image
scribed on the walls his heart
Throughout all the turns of events that transpired while we
were apart and since coming back together
I don't know whether to thank them for thinking he saw me
in such a way that back then he didn't feel worthy, but
knows he's a better man today
Or should I curse them for the oversight that led him astray?

Nevertheless, what those eyes beheld led him back to
holding me- those eyes captured my spirit and set my soul
free
Now it's impossible to look upon each other sweet bitterly
cause we now look at everything so differently
It's never been more clear to me that so much is derived
from imagery
The way they envisioned me after such a brief walk once
upon a time with me
brought us to this moment where a simple talk feels like
a fantasy
A welcomed recurring nostalgic dream only we're wide
awake living out each scene
and life now bursts at the seams with all the joy,
contentment and hope each sunrise brings
When I look at you, I see me
When you look at me, you see we
Us setting trails ablaze as the world becomes amazed by all
the stereotypes we'll challenge
and fulfill possibilities that you and I have always imagined
Those eyes looked into my heart in love after so many
looked upon just to scold her
and I found myself in love again with the beauty within
the eyes of the beholder

1/23/21
{For PooBonny}

11

Get Angry

I wanna be angry
For all that has lead up to this very moment
For every minute you plundered from my happiness
Every time I suppressed my real feelings about who you
really are or how poorly you treated me
I want to be angry
For always forcing me to these extremes
For giving up or wasting away my dreams due to your
insecurities or lack of support
How you can so easily distort the sincerest of intentions
Not to mention the way you make me question and
second guess my own sanity
The way you turn things around and get mad at me for my
valid reasons to be
Angry
You make me so mad and I want so badly to stay stuck
on these feelings that have me wanting to hate you
Wishing I never had the notion to date you
Asking God did He create you and I to be the source of
each other's karma
Because of the drama we gave others and ultimately
returned on ourselves
But it's all your fault, no it's mine
We're both the blame for all the time that we can't get
back
With all this incessant and childish tic for tac
For all the emotional maturity you lack
And my vindictive need to strike back
With the cruelest attack on your manhood
Not allowing for consideration that we may have

misunderstood the intent
That what was said or done or lied about wasn't meant to destroy
only to decoy or distract me from someone else
Someone who was willing to love me more than himself
Someone who knew he'd wed me if given the chance
Someone capable of showing me true romance
Thinking on the chances I gave up for you only enhances my desire to be livid
Damn the memories are so vivid
I still remember the first day we met 18 years ago
the numerous times since then that I've wondered should I stay or should I go
The sporadic weeks, months, or years that we'd spend apart
Only to come back together still holding each other's heart for ransom
You've always been so handsome
A soothing sight for sore eyes
Wearing the inconspicuous disguise of someone who knew how to love
Hiding behind enchanting neo soul music and sentimental memories
Calls, messages, and Kama Sutra degrees of sexuality, love making, fucking, earth shaking, weak in the knees, licking, sucking, pulling, smacking, swallowing, wallowing, follow and unfollowing, friend and unfriending, block and unblocking, clocking, stalking, walking, talking, fussing, fighting, cussing, writing, break up, make up, stuck, YOU NAME IT
We did that shit to each other
Friends turned lovers to arch enemies
And you wonder why I wanna be so angry

Things change so quickly between us
From pillow talk between the sheets to barely a greeting
of good morning the next day
Looking at me like you're disgusted when I feel the exact
same way
Yet and still I retract demanding you to leave and beg
you to stay
Because I can't ever bare for us to end that way
All mad and upset saying things we only mean temporarily
Or maybe deep down it's ordinarily how anyone would
feel in the same situation
After the buildup of relentless frustration
From the tremendous dedication I had to loving you
despite the cycle of devastation we seem to constantly
repeat
And now I'm staring into the depths of defeat
Exhausted and drained feeling every ounce of pain and
regret because it's still not over yet
Nevertheless this weariness is no longer met with
bitterness
That's why no matter how much I want to be I just can't
get angry anymore
Finally accepting that better things are in store for the
both of us
If we just stop holding on to nothing we could grab hold
of something substantial
Something intangible that we hold inside
That will release all of our foolish pride and unnecessary
fears of trust and vulnerability
Our heart and soul truly wants to be free
Fallacies of shoulds are what keeps you and me from
loving one another unconditionally

Instead of pointing out what's wrong with you and what's
not right with me
We could've easily allowed ourselves to be perfect for
each other
We could've discovered who we were meant to be, rather
than me hoping in the potential of what I see in you
and you tearing down the high standards you once held
me to
There's no need to dwell on our failures and mistakes
I just needed to take one final moment to get this all off
my chest because I wanna be so mad but my anger has
regressed
Not overwhelmed with sorrow, but melancholy at best
Letting go of the brokenness but clinging the rest of
what's left of my being
Praying that I'll finally start seeing the wholeness of the
beautiful mess we made of this fiery passion we share
A sacred bond that will always be there
This undying love for you that makes me no longer care...
to get angry

9/24/18

Inheritance

So this is what you left-
the anguish of men who love me but are unwilling to
stay
The lack of ability to show me but it's so thrilling to say
you always did
From the time when I was only a kid
like the game, I hid all my emotions like a treasure to
find
the pain that I buried deep inside my mind
Now they're all blinded to the notion that I live
and breathe to share all I have to give
Still what is it worth when it feels like nothing
Making too much out of something that was never
meant to be
Like your relationship with me
and my brothers and sisters
Replaced by empty romances with ladies and misters
While you kept writing letters telling *her* you missed her
Just leave my mama alone
Oh, you already did that when she was barely grown
Trying to make ends meet with all these mouths to feed
while you could've cared less that she was in need
So this is what you left us-
Confused about who and what to trust
Misled by false promises, hopes and dreams
Sown on smiles bursting at the seams
of despair

I never felt like I wanted you there
Never thought I needed to care
And that's how I learned to carry the rest
Never giving my heart, but my body at best
So much easier to lay down
than to hope for them to stay around
You taught me that men are just a means to an end
Dead end, dep-end, the end and like the wind
Gone
Never has there been one that I could always count on
But countless the times I've been done wrong
I'm not gonna sing this sad love song
I've inflicted my illness onto others
Friends who dared to become lovers
Tried so hard to fill my emptiness with fleeting moments
of happiness
Until the bliss wore off and they were left with me
Starved for attention, just wanting to be
someone's choice, his one and only
Chosen over other woman or worldly vices
To simply adore me as if I were priceless
And I know this kind of love exists
because I've seen it in glimpses of others' lives
Faithful husbands and devoted wives
Children who had the privilege of a mother and father
Step-folk who stepped up when biological didn't bother
And though I was only looking in as an outsider
The image sure looked good with him right beside her

That life must not be what is meant
Because even after trying with the purest intent
I counted all the wasted time I spent trying to give my
family the same look
The promise of forever when all it took was a day to all
be over
How I gave so much of myself until he drove *her* away
That little girl inside of me who liked to play
With the idea of being loved unconditionally
Unorthodoxed yet traditionally
One woman-one man-one family
But seemingly, I can't find one man who genuinely
Carries all these traits so usually I need three
Like a divine trinity I need him for love, him for trust,
and him for raw passion and lust
I need him to stay in case the other leaves
and when he's gone the other helps me grieve
And as each of them meets a different need
I realize that I am broken
fragmented as each word spoken in different dialect
That's when I'm reminded of your neglect
So this is what you left me- regret.

4/27/16

Poetic Interludes: Inspiration

I need some inspiration
Motivation for hire!
Ignite a fire burning with lyrical greatness
Render me breathless
Until my only word left is...

Evolution

- If you believe in evolution then you're already halfway to a full understanding of what I am about to say.
- Humans cannot give birth to monkeys, nor monkeys to humans as thus; but from the earth's sands and a breath is how God created us.
- It was not His intention for us to remain the same, but through experience and growth we would eventually change.
- So it's my advice to you to take heed to these things and acknowledge the significance that evolution brings.
- Long ago the races learned separately if even at all. Now education is offered equally to beings great and small.
- We are now so comfortable with the people we daily meet, not having to call anyone "Master" before we speak.
- Yet, for everything that looks good there is always something more, like the lack of family unity that there was before.
- When we used to all have a hand in raising our children right, now raise a hand to someone else's child and the parents are ready to fight.
- We are no longer offended by the use of the word "nigger", but innocent people are still dying and it's our children pulling the trigger.
- The generations have changed, but is it really for the best? We need to build on the positive and do away with the rest.

- Like the rise of independent women who work so hard to not feel intimidated by men and can let down their guard.
- I read an article questioning if Black History is still necessary. Evidently inspired by the envy of our adversary.
- However, there was still a solid point made, we should honor achievements of the past as well as today.
- Nevertheless, evolution is not just about the significant changes between the races, but also the change in each individual whose mirror has two faces.
- Like the girl who went through childhood with low self-esteem, who now settles for nothing less than being treated as a queen.
- Or the bullying thug who couldn't tell you the meaning of a verb, who is now an intellectual scholar and a teacher of God's word.
- During the trials of life we all go through many phases, and some type of epiphany is reached in each of its stages.
- They say with each new day something new is learned. So search for new ways to get over those bridges of opportunity we burned.
- If we step outside the box we'll see the barriers quickly dissolve, and how we'll view the world much differently the more we evolve.
- For every problem we face we'll realize there is a solution, and maybe we'll strive to find the answers together now that we know the truth about evolution.   2004

It's Not You; *It's Me*

It's not you, it's me;
This ain't just a lame excuse- you see
I was so hung up on trying to figure out if he just wanted to
use me
why he claims to love me, but still won't choose me
And then like lightening reality struck
a jolt so frightening I was like WTF
Where and when did I lose my mind
forget that I'm cut from cloths of the Divine
another queen like me he'll never find
But that's not what he was looking for anyway
his type is more like sophisticatedly rachet
And those 2 things don't even go together
but he must not think much of himself to want better
Still it wasn't his fault that I fell for the game
His words, actions, and wit aren't to blame
what I chose to accept kind of put me to shame
I put up this front acting like I didn't care
that I was partaking of someone else's share
blocking out the truth like *she* wasn't really there
He talked about her like she was irrelevant
until I took note of all the time he spent
bringing up their problems, how she is so crazy,
stupid, dumb, worthless and lazy
But that's who he chose to go home to each night
To keep the peace and make things right
So he'd always have a place to rest his head
while he made pit stops from bed to bed
But like I said, it's not you- it's me
Waiting for you to be with just me
I had to be the one to set myself free

See it for what it was and take responsibility
No need to be mad and act like he was wrong
when I knew what I was getting all along
If he could disrespect her for not meeting his needs
When he's usually up to no good deeds
How was my faithful patience perceived
My persistence to somehow make him change
His resistance for his situation to be rearranged
This may sound strange but I truly commend her
for putting up with behaviors most wouldn't prefer
For accepting him when she knows he's unfaithful
and takes care of him when he's so ungrateful
She may yell, argue, and say obscene things
but at the end of the day she has everything
That up until this point I thought I wanted
that ultimately would've left me disappointed
Honestly, I know there's no need to compare
what I have to offer to what he gets over there
I know in the beginning he longed for my touch
probably never has loved anyone else as much
Until I started to resemble his home life such
as making demands for his time
forgetting that he's not even mine
questioning him about who he texts and sees
worried about him putting it on anyone else but me
I was blinded to the only one of real concern
The one for who he denies that he truly yearns
So I take this as a lesson learned
No salty tears or sad goodbyes
Just walk away with my head held high
He asked me why this is how it has to be
I just smiled and said, it's not you- it's me   3/11/16

More Than Words

Words cannot describe
Theory could never explain
The triumph in loss, the defeat of gain
Pain's joy, joy's pain
All-encompassing with a warrior's spirit that can never be
conquered
Nostalgic thoughts, present day dreams, moments of ponder, what if
and   I wonder
That unspoken bond, reciprocated vow between I knew it was
meant to be and I can't even see how
A sacred gift to hold within, yet abundant when given out
Oblivious obsession
Dances with destiny
Fancies fate
Without there'd be no life worth living without
Inspires inspiration
Encourages courage
Beauty beyond vision
Sight unseen
A screaming whisper
A silent cry
They call it wrong-right, they call it right-wrong, but it's the only
thing right left
Is it right that it never left
Is it wrong that it's still feels right
You, me, you and me, you and she, he and me, she and she, he and
he, they and we all fall
And rise and plunge and dive and tread, and dread and yearn
Fear its return, anticipate its departure
Warm salutations welcoming in
Cold goodbyes escorting out
And as the door closes behind the draft it leaves the essence of
your memory
4-1-14

Premonition

I wish I could turn down my clairvoyance
Ignore my intuition
Turn a blind eye and a deaf ear to the premonition of
the words I haphazardly wanted to hear to validate
my fears
Drown out the sounds I wish I could forget
the nostalgia in the way she remembered the day
they both met
The day that would lead to unwarranted hurt and
regret
I wish our pasts didn't foreshadow this turn of events
causing me to presently speak of him in past
tense because I haven't been the same since hearing
her story
The blaze of glory they quickly became, floated high
up in smoke then crashed and burned in the flames
I knew it when I saw her name
casually notified by the phone, the text he hoped to
see alone, but it was meant for me to catch that
vision
and now I'm faced with the decision of should I stay
or should I go
Should I pretend like I don't know or front like I don't
care that my man got caught up in her young
intrigued stare
A gaze so deep it penetrated the Facebook and IG
page, solidified the sentiment of the posts as he
started to do the most with comments and emojis;
how he pursued her like he subdued me, so

persistent and blatantly that she didn't wait to see
that he was already taken
Still, it was only he who was mistaken thinking he
could forsake the love he'd been making and creating
with me
Right when we started to feel like a family he jumped
out of the family tree
and tried to use an olive branch extended as a lifeline
only after I found out
but this shadow of doubt had been cast long before
I wanted nothing more than to believe that we could
withstand the unbreakable habits of a broken man or
mend the pieces of this scorned torn woman
I thought love would prevent him from needing to
feel the thrill of the chase
I begged him to stop running while looking back
because it's then where one starts to lack the
momentum to keep moving forward
He'd end up running towards the reasons why I met
him lonely
The reason he so eagerly made me his one and only,
only his eyes were never solely for me
As much as he could see his life changing for the
better with me, I always felt that to a degree it still
was not enough
Ironically, I never truly felt like he belonged to me,
yet we were undeniably connected
He called me friend, his wonder twin, so I can't figure
out when the bond was no longer felt
When he decided that the pleasing of self was more

gratifying than the pleasure he derived having
someone who genuinely cared by his side
He had so much pride before his fall. Stood tall on the
notion that this new feeling wouldn't be revealed and
if uncovered could be healed through my addictive
desire for him
He didn't imagine that the chances would be slim that
I'd forgive him
Or maybe he fathomed that he'd be better off
without me. Wild and free thoughts of her made him
see commitment differently.
Leading to the breaking of the biggest promise he
ever made to me that no matter what he'd always be
faithful to me
Others can say it was just sex and it makes me so
vexed as to ignore the carelessness of his ways. How
he went on for days, weeks, and months thereafter
craving the sound of her laughter and the smell of her
skin. How he told her how good he felt within his
heart
while he could've cared less that I would fall apart at
the knowledge of him now knowing her in a way I
tried to prevent
By simply asking him to end the side bar secret
conversations, emotionally driven lamentations that
led to sexual sensations that begged for a
demonstration
He gave in to the temptation that was really his
mission and altered reality to give himself permission
to do whatever he wanted

Did he forget he flaunted our relationship for all to see, did he think she wouldn't find out about me? Did he assume she already knew?

Either way, for the lengths he went through and the chances he took he committed fraud and became love's crook, stole my heart and her dignity that upon a deeper look she never would've given a second glance to partake in another woman's romance

Now I wish I can turn up my clairvoyancy. Look into the future to find out what he really sees in me before I let his empty pleas for me fill me once again with hope

Will I live to regret him or move on and forget him? All I know is I can't unsee the image of him with someone else outside of the open pleasure we shared between ourselves

I can't erase the fact that he went behind my back after repeated lies he'd have to retract when her truth was told and my heart went cold and this game became old because I choose to no longer bend and fold the things I know I know

For it is he who must be blind, deaf, and dumb to hurt the only one he was ever motivated to be a better man for and there may be no way to even the score because all love is lost when trust is no more and I should've considered this before he did exactly what I knew he'd do by not heeding the warning of my third eye vision of the reality that came from my premonition   11/3/20

Speechless...

I feel like my words no longer hold weight
but the connotation is heavy enough to sink the Titanic
knowing I've said too much, now I hesitate
throwing my weary heart into a fear induced panic
wondering if this is the end
No apologetic phrases to defend
all the terrible things my actions said
Boasting loud believing I had all the facts
when in reality it was all make believe
in hindsight pulling my vocal chords to retract
the unwarranted attack that forced you to leave
And in that moment I didn't care
but the anguish in your stare
was the keynote speech on betrayal
Trembling as if nerves overtook your steps
still strong enough not to break stride
although I had sank into the lowest depths
my inflated ego couldn't reach your pride
That's when I knew I was wrong
but I've been used to fighting so long
that my thoughts dwell in the trenches
Accusations flying like first strike in war
I became the terrorist that I myself feared
unbeknownst to the protective image I bore
through open wounds deep insecurities peered
and suddenly I'm in soliloquy
battling the enemy within me
Desperately waving the white flag
Talking myself down attempting to negotiate

with the irrational demands I place on your heart
coming to terms with the pointless debate
that nearly ripped our lives apart
Ironically at a loss for words
new ones you just haven't heard
that could erase all your sorrow
Realizing there is nothing I could possibly say
maybe very few things still left to do
to alter the series of fateful events today
and reconnect the fragments of what we've been through
II just sit in quiet reflection
emotions in boisterous objection
to the initial opening statement
Self-inflicted subjection to be muted
until the content of my character aligns with the thesis
rendering signs that my devotion is undisputed
that only you'll be able to still hear- when I'm speechless

4/8/17

PoliTICKing

These worldviews and ideologies of the many and few are
so misty eyed and muggy that it's hard to see through to
the clear picture
As if the perspective isn't skewed by rituals,
traditions, beliefs, facts and fiction, contradictions
and rewritten scriptures
Please tell me what you see
We could be staring at the exact same thing and see
NOthing alike and then feel like our light is dimmed
because you didn't agree with her and I didn't agree
with him that the outlook is either hopeful or grim
Tell me what your stance is on giving second chances to
those who in different circumstances may have seen and
acted on the reflection of one's own experience and the
influence couldn't be fluently translated
Is it possible for some parts of history to become
outdated instead of ambiguously weighted against present
day extremes
The scales are unbalanced whenever one's personal
opinion is taken as a challenge and is left to feel like
having one is miniscule if it doesn't follow the crowd
Just cause you shout yours loud or you speak it proud
doesn't mean that those who humbly bow in understanding
aren't commanding the same respect
How easily we forget that we're all in the same boat
where negativity flies as hope floats meanwhile those in
white coats, black cloaks, red or blue wing tips
continue to narrate the script while telling us to get a
grip as they flip lives like a coin toss over monetary
gain versus lives lost
While we count a cost that can't ever be equally
measured still we fight to value and treasure our kind
above the rest instead of recognizing the best in the
whole of mankind— It's like the fear of being colorblind

is going to erase the entire palette of origins of the
indigenous man or the history of our motherland
On the other hand, those CONdescending from the Caucasus
hold caucuses to choose whose more fit to lead and rule
by majority and deceive us into thinking there's a
minority in those of the same human species.
Feeding us a load of feces about us being a cursed
people when we know the root of all evil stems from the
lack of melanin in their skin and there's very little
light sinking in, yet causing us to continually burn in
their hell
Left to rot in jail cells or suddenly dying by inhales
of airborne genocide
Oh the many ways they've tried to make us extinct
Always acting before they think and in the blink of an
eye a Black life is on the brink of meeting it's maker
at the hands of bylaw makers, hooded haters, uniformed
reapers and false prophet teachers and when we cry out
Teacher! There are things I don't wanna learn cause the
last one I had told me lies, they laugh at our loved
ones cries from being forced to say goodbye without
reason
Begging and pleading to stop being beaten, taking a knee
against being kneed in the neck til we're no longer
breathing
Tell me what's the defense against being born in
Black skin
Where's the offense in natural born dominance that is so
undeniably evident that at first glance it's decided
that we don't deserve a chance to survive
No equal opportunity to thrive on the land we plowed and
tilled, using our knowledge and skill against our wills
to fulfill their need to make us feel less than
When there's obviously no comparison yet we've always
been the better man they programmed to turn the other
cheek as they slap criminalization on the meek, fear
among the weak and dehumanize our inhumanly strong

32

Now, America stands on the brink of a Swan Song
beyond nuclear annihilation they've created a hesitation
to breathe freely after denying the right to speak
freely only if we start speaking on the rights they
easily violate through the motive of hate
As the world lays in wait for change, we partake of all
this strange fruit being grown without roots, reproduced
with no seeds, cuts of meat that don't bleed
Fill the shelves with cheap junk and then accuse us of
greed as it's consumed rapidly cause we always assume
that one day soon there won't be anything left to eat
Subjectively becoming hoarders,
collecting baggage of the forefathers' kidnapping of our
ancestors and now children of men are storing live stock
at the borders
Meanwhile, whole communities are struggling to keep
their head above water after keeping their head above
the rising waters that have destroyed it time and
time again
Either we rise or we sink from the contaminated waters
from our sinks all the poison they force us to drink has
failed to take away some of our ability to think
for ourselves
They continually dwell on how to make us extinct
Instead we're on the brink of a revolution, minds
becoming in sync with the ancient scribes of evolution
that starts with minds changed, rearranged after going
insane, it's like we're being inadvertently trained
for war
Just like before when the few of many couldn't take no
more and took matters into their own hands we shall
reclaim our lands beyond 50 acres and a mule
Drop bombs on the confederate romanTICK
using the quick draw McGraw anTICK
debating truth with probable semanTICK
Of poli-TICK-TICK BOOM!
4/2/21

33

One Day...

There's something to be noted in the distance that
is exaggerated in the resistance of one day-
One day without fulfilling the desire of just
hearing you say, "Hey, have a great day."
One day without seeing you smile from ear to ear
with a sentiment both charming and sincere
warming my heart and other more hidden parts
of me
Admitting that your night ended and morning
began with adorning thoughts of me
Intimately, passionately, not in the usual
fashion that we try to engage casually to prevent
casualties of the heart
Denying that the breakdown of walls has begun
to start because in just one day apart
It was evident that we're more than friends
It's getting harder to pretend yet easier to defend
my need for you to listen to the pain that I go
through and then assure me that I'll always
have a friend in you; and likewise
At times I hear your heart's cries as your gaze
penetrates my eyes while you press all life's

pressures between my thighs

I know you can feel the relief as I pour all my grief in an explosive secretion of appreciation

For the sensation of being desired from the inflation of each other's ego and descension of intention to stop although we know that this amusing ride just leads to nowhere

Still some days we're too high to even care, too right to even dare focus on our fate

The way we relate can't possibly be a mistake, the laughter, the trust, the love we make that in the wake of it causes my emotions to retreat

Fearfully retract those 3 words from speech when in soliloquy I speak them freely hoping you can feel me every time my hellos really mean

I Love You

When the request to be in your space is more so to just see your face, get lost in your embrace, and carelessly let down my guard

I realized in just one day that it's so hard to get through the hours without you

As I sit here writing this poem about you I can't help but wonder what you're going through and what made

us both decide today to resist the willingness to be
in bliss
To reminisce about our last moment in mind when
I imagined I was yours and you were mine in a
land before time played our hands and life cards
were already dealt
Surmising that everything that is felt between
us must be telekinetically expressed leading these
emotional highs to suddenly digress into valleys of
trying to remember not to forget that the
circumstances in which our plight is met is the
union of our regret
Nevertheless, in just one day I realized that you
make every day feel like Sunday, as I bask in
hope's light and wallow in the strategically
repressed dreams that maybe one day...

and I said all that to say that today, I really
missed you

10/1/20

In Deep Thought...

You remind me of something I've never had;
a familiar nostalgic feeling between my hopes for the
future and my despairing past
Suspended right there in the balance of time spins an
array of colorful thoughts of you on my mind
Staring down a kaleidoscope of the distorted beauty of an
honesty that is so new to me,
the things you do to me without your own knowledge or
intent-
allowing you to explore the depths of my being with full
consent
Your touch is the warmth of my imagination
Your kiss, a cooling sensation for the temperate vibes you
release in conversation
The moistening of my desire fills the atmosphere with
pheromones stimulated by the scent of your cologne and
the idea of us alone
You've had me in so many ways,
as I close my eyes and daydream or wander in an
enchanting gaze
All I see is everything I've ever wanted
and you becoming all that and more
If only you were free to explore beyond the limits of the
moment
If only I wasn't confounded to the infatuation of
wonderment
for these beautiful present memories of something I've
never had...   6/4/19

The Birds and the Bees

This feeling is the most immensely profound pain I've ever felt; it's like combining all the losses from the cards that were dealt every time I took a gamble on love. Everything that I was once so sure of is now confusion at its finest. Pick up a bee in kindness and learn it's limitations, only the sting is just a reaction to unfamiliar surroundings and situations. That protective venom it holds inside is so toxic that it literally commits suicide in defense of one's self- believing I was the enemy when I was only trying to help. This immensely profound pain pours from my weary eyes and releases all my broken heart's cries as my body begins to react to the impact of his fear. So innocent the way our paths crossed in circles we randomly flew near. The flowers in the meadow created a warm glow around a creature who doesn't even know or understand his own nature. His purpose for existence as simple as the nomenclature; to just be[e]. He doesn't realize as he prances from flower to flower looking to devour that sweet nectar that he's leaving behind trails of life that avails us to believe in the process. Now viewing the field of erect roses and ingesting the taste of golden sweet honey as progress, I was enticed to dive deep between the petals to indulge in the same flower beds with him. In greed and selfishness, we drank down to the stem and rested our gluttonous desires on weak limbs dangling from the tree of life. I followed as he continued to elude me, until he began to get used to my company. Allowing us to drink side by side while still guarded by his pride. Yet I saw he had such a vast need to be fulfilled and it became my thrill to bring him his flowers. Hours turned to days, sunshine turned to rain, and then the seasons changed so drastically. In the coldness of winter he disappeared and I prayed he'd find his way back to me in spring. Until one day his tiny wings gave way to the weight of his insatiable hunger and the nectar monger fell towards the ground. I came swooning in to rescue him and this is when I found the limit. He'd forgotten all the times I joined him in it. I noticed him growing in stature, appearing stronger to the naked eye. Yet, when he glanced upon my similarly changing features he saw me as a different creature and tried to fly-- away. I begged of him to remember all the days before November when I gave him my devotion, discovering now that my valiant efforts were lost on the false notion that it was meant for us to coexist simultaneously. It was only intended for us to survive life in the same place, not to reside in the same space ideally. Sharing such a strong passion and coitus thirst at first seemed like a perfect match. Twins fraternal where hope springs eternal within the inner child of this boy and girl, just trying to make a real connection in this cruel and lonely world. Our intense appetites was the deepest level by which we came to know one another, although it was apparent that I wanted us to be much more than just lovers. So naturally, I took this final chance to extend grace to this evidently weak being I thought was a friend. Before realizing that it was me, his defenses met my rescue offensively and we fell so hard from that apple tree. Descending in slow motion suspended we lay lifelessly as he uttered the faintness of an apology for not recognizing me sooner. Watching like an outer body experience as the betrayal consumed her unable to aid because he too is now dying while realizing she was only trying to help. Life flashing before him and no guard left as his innate defensive measures deplete the treasure for the first time felt is understanding that I followed him in love, that I fed him so eagerly seeking to destroy his urge to flee. Now the pain swells inside of me for loving him in spite of me. Believing since we both had wings that he was supposed to fly alongside me: I, the ravenous bird and he the killer bee. Wisdom in hindsight of the verge of death and all that's left is the memory. Looking for healing power in flowers that seem familiar only now the taste is peculiar and met with bitterness. The nectar will never be as sweet as when we drank together in beautiful weather on sunny days. We part ways in a foggy haze trying to make night and day of what happened. Who was the real antagonist in this plot twist? Was it the free bird's naive willingness to find the connection in all things, or the honeybee's guarded nature to defensively sting? All I know is that this lesson is more than just about the birds and the bees but learning how it's easy to be deceived by our own wants and needs and how our truest nature is reflected in words and deeds. Sometimes we don't understand what we're doing until it's all said and done. Sometimes we lose ourselves in the thoughts of many when we only really needed that one to show us a reflection of the way we're living- to teach us lessons in forgiving and how to dwell in harmony while respecting human nature's boundaries. So, from this immensely profound pain and metaphoric death I know this bird will rise again and the truest part left of that bee will always   remain   inside   of   me.

1/13/21

P.T.S.D.: Put That Shit Down

So this is how it ends-
Ironically, spiraling back to where it all began is where I
recognized the cycle
A **P**ain **T**remendously **S**adistically **D**isheartening is how I
describe the symptoms of **PTSD**
See, **P**ost **T**raumatic **S**tress **D**isorder encompasses so many
things
People think it's only sparked by wars and things of that nature
However, I've fallen victim to the disease in all its
interchangeable nomenclature-
and since I'm a writer, it's only befitting that I
Put **T**hat **S**hit **D**own on paper
I got an official diagnosis
Underwent all the psychological testing and treatments
possible, except for hypnosis
although I've tried to trick my brain into doing something other
than what my heart wanted
tried to see what wasn't there; like a mirage in the desert, the
image of him and I together taunted me
We had a **P**hysically **T**oxic **S**exual **D**ependency, getting our fix
off so many others
Our hidden addiction bonded us as lovers as we loved to love
each other from the dramatic way we'd **P**ut **T**hat **S**hit **D**own on
one another
I mean, the thrill of falling back in was greater than being with
People **T**hat **S**tayed **D**own
Having them around consistently never felt the same way it felt
when I knew *he* missed me
No matter how many times he dissed me, the way he kissed
me when we made up made me
Perpetuate **T**he **S**ame **D**ysfunction
Childhood is where we first malfunctioned

Abuse, neglect, and rejection were normal feelings and we
never really knew how much we needed healing until we
started dealing with
Psychological Tumultuous Stress Differentials
Comparing our pain and making the likeness sentimental; this
is how we became detrimental to ourselves
Me carrying denial of daddy issues and him seeking the love
he should've gotten from his mamma, it's no wonder we never
got   Past The Stupid Drama of manipulation and control
He wanted to own my soul and I wanted to stop feeling like he
stole my heart
tossed it way up in the sky and watched as it fell apart
He didn't try to protect me from the impact
In fact, it was his favorite part of our tic for tac
Wondering each time how I'd react when he reached out his
hand to pull me back in
I would defend all the terrible things he did to me saying I was
arguably the same-
that I had also done things to warrant his pain
Still, I was his sunshine after the rain
Me loving him unconditionally made him proudly want to reign
over me
and his power was my authority
Historically, I was always in control, but truth be told it was all
an illusion
Plausible Truth Summoned Delusion for everything I wanted
to believe
I couldn't fathom or conceive that we weren't meant to be
We were bonded eternally, he pledged his undying love for me
and that was enough
the words were evidently filled with fluff because they didn't
hold weight when times got tough and he got going
Leaving me so easily, knowing I'd be awaiting his return

Well, this time I finally learned
because the unexpected pleasure of someone else actually
loving me, triggered my **PTSD**
This new man provides me with all the things I said I want,
need, and deserve,
but I have the nerve to still pine over you
After all the relentless trauma we put each other through and
finally finding a means of escape
This super man swooped in with his cape and lifted me from
the gallows of self-hate
Although, we've been inseparable since our first date, I fear it
may be too late to save me from the irreparable damage of
wading in shallow waters in wait for another trigger
to start the cycle again of falling back in love with the familiar
because this old-new feeling is so foreign that I'm afraid it
might feel boring without all the heart wrenching emotional pull
My heart should be full of hope, gratefulness, and desire for
the one who has so reinspired my faith in man,
but I don't know if I can or should trust it beyond the what ifs
and the unknown
What if a place in this new heart isn't my home
If I would've known that healthy love would be clouded with so
much doubt then I'd have much rather done without-
and that's how the disorder works in **P**eople **T**hat **S**hut **D**own at
the promise of tomorrow
Waking up feeling like you're on borrowed time
Wondering if I'm the only one on his mind
Wondering when our time will be up and I'll be left stuck feeling
alone again
and find myself seeking out the one friend who undisguised is
my enemy
The devil I knew was not a real friend to me

I was more comfortable with that reality than not knowing what
potentially could or couldn't be
I'm sick of being obsessed with this dysfunctionality that's so
contradicting to my winning personality
Yet, I downplay my clairvoyant sensibility-
drown my pain in Pills, Thrills, Sex and Drugs.... and the worst
and greatest of these is love
Love is the only cure for what ails us
the treatment for the lack of trust that life goes on and gets
better
The fact that down to the letter, I write
Poetry That Saves Dreams
to help me cope with the overflow of emotions bursting at the
seams
When it seems stress is all I'm destined for, I realize there's so
much more in store for me
Once I take the road less traveled, allow myself to get lost, and
lose the tendency to count the cost of yearning for something I
never really had
I will embark upon Positive Transcendental Self-Discovery
and the uncovering of the mysterious love that evaded me will
enable me to live a life that is more profound
now that I understand that the only way to truly let all this
post-traumatic stress go is to
Put That Shit Down!

2/12/20

45

Poetic Interludes: Affirmation

Let my love heal you-
May the reflective light in me shine to reveal
God in you
Let my wisdom be the manifestation of your
dreams-
As we reclaim our ancestral rule as kings
and queens
As the seasons change and social climate
vastly shifts-
May my devotion to only you remain your
most treasured gift

12/2015

Forget to Remember

I never saw my father put hands on my mother
Heard the stories of the way he beat her and my oldest brother
Guess I was just too young to remember...
It's funny how I still have memories of other things back then
Like the drunken stench of that raggedy ass nasty old man who
liked to lay hands on my big sister and I
Like how I learned at such a tender age how to hold in my cry
Cause that's what they were after
The thrill of inflicting pain to take away a child's laughter
Strange how I can recall
The preying stares of my friend's uncles and daddies
Who found ways to inconspicuously grab me
And grope and grind before I was nine
It's no wonder that little boys AND girls
Felt drawn to me like an anomaly
Exploring the anatomy the way the grownups did it-- to us
But chastised and shamed if we were ever caught
Adding insult to injury
To the fact that everyone who touched me were of some relation
or affiliation to family
Until that one time when those gang members raped me and my
now late bestie
Thank God it wasn't just me
So many of us walking around wearing scars no one else can see
So many cast down their judgment of me
Those who don't even know me are so full of envy
Trying to figure out why their man wants me

Convincing themselves that he was just fucking me
When in actuality he really fucked with me
Cause I learned how to take giving a fuck to another level
Them sick ass child molesting and rapist devils taught me a thing
or two
I never made my life about what I've been through
People closest to me never even knew and there are still a few
who may just be learning
What they perceived as lustful yearning
Was to me a means of control
Take my body but not my soul
When allowed to enter my body it was a union of broken spirited
souls
The weakest got buried below the many
The strongest barely survive friendship and think its destiny
To have met someone like me
This quick witted, sometimes pretending to be dim witted, dumbed
down yet thumbs up personality
Be having the most aloof of men stuck
This one dude scornfully named me the black widow
But affectionately called me the mentalist
Said he peeped how I be bodying niggas and he didn't wanna be the
next one on the list
But he was really feelin this vibe, the deep emotional connection
we shared
Then like the others he dared and got scared when I sapiosexed
his mind
Claimed he loved me but it was just a bad time
For a woman like me he just wasn't ready
Until I decided to go steady with another

Now he's enticed to be my secret lover
And though as kids he was my biggest crush
I no longer have time for these childish games
Thinking it's the sex that keeps them is why some people are so
lame
That's why I perfected my head game
Its seems to all be one in the same
Childhood sexual trauma caused early carnal knowledge increase
Hypersexuality became a means of stress release
Got em thinking she's gotta have it every day
Until I finally figured out what made me this way
Channeled the negative energy and painful memories
Turned them into life lessons and various degrees of education
From enduring the depths of unwarranted devastation
To the self-proclaimed declaration that
I AM A QUEEN
Which has been proven to mean that
I turn street fighters into soldiers willing to defend my honor
Help self-doubting girls understand that it should be an honor just
to hold their hand
That even if their virtue was once stolen they don't have to keep
willingly giving it away
That even after a lifetime of dark nights they can still hope for
brighter days
Teach boys and man-child alike how to live like responsible adults
Hoping to minimize the stats of domestic violence and sexual
assault
Hoping to increase the awareness of its prevalence
And to expose the secrecy of its indecency
There are kings and queens walking among us living as peasants

Fed the awful lies about the value of their presence
There is no greater treasure than the discovery of one's own worth
No measure to uncovering the purpose of your birth
So even as you like I may ponder on hurtful things
Don't forget to remember the satisfaction that it brings
To look at how far you've come from where you've been
And find yourself walking with the greatest of them
Although I never saw my father put hands on my mother
I learned that a man who does harm a woman can't possibly love her
And that even if she loves him, she has to love herself more
To pick up her self-respect and walk out the door
Men and women alike learned to stay quiet when adversity struck
But while trying to forget the past remember that it's never too late to speak up
And though for years no one knew I bore the burden of sexual abuse and domestic violence
I pray that many lives will be saved simply from breaking my silence

Don't forget to remember...
#Herstoryismystory
#Mystoryisyourstory

Break the Silence... Domestic Violence and Child Sexual Abuse Awareness

5/6/18

Thinking Out Loud...

What a difference a day, let alone 10 years makes... and I can't really say it was worth the wait cause being with you again felt like no time had ever passed since the last time you were all up in this...

Asking how does it feel and how do I want it cause your sex game is the truth and you know how to flaunt it... Had me feeling all types of ways, didn't know which way was up... Speaking that text talk like OMG WT...

Phonetic sounds ringing from my mouth like opera music when you found that spot and worked hard not to lose it... Sweat poured like rain as you swam through my seas and gripped my mountains so firmly while I was on my...

Needless to say, you put it down that night and something about it just always feels right even though it's so wrong that we never pretend that this will ever amount to love in the...

Endurance, stamina, physically you have it all, but one thing I've learned by now is that I'd be crazy to fall cause you never allow yourself to attach to just one chick and I'm just one of many who get all caught up in loving your...

Diction and words that you speak so kind assuring that you're truly a friend of mine... But you've always had your situations and I've had mine, too, and at the end of the day I'm just not that into...

You know I'm lying cause you so damn fine and

lately you're the first and last thought on my mind
But I'm trying to stay grounded as I keep moving
closer to the edge with every thrust of your warm
body between my...
Ledge scaling now trying so hard to hold on, to save
face for the fact that now I'm so gone... Off the way
that you give it so good and plenty and how I've
come to crave the feeling of you coming in...
Mediocre would never describe the experience of
you and all I can say is god damn this dude... He just
don't know what he's doing to me, feeling like Jagged
Edge singing *I gotta...*
Believe that it just is what it is; he'll never be mine
and I'll never be his... No matter how close what we
do starts to feel like romance we're both always too
afraid to take that...
Chances are there'd be too many issues with trust
cause we've always had so much *ish* with us and
maybe what happens between us wouldn't be so
profound if we made the obligation to be tied...
Downer Debbie let me get out of my feelings cause
my words have already been too revealing and it's
probably written all over my face every time I end up
back in his...
Space and time never too far in between, but I'm
getting too old to wonder what it means we used to
blame it on the fact that we were young, but we're a
decade older now and this still feels dumb;
that I accept the fact that I want you but I'm too
scared to have you cause you give it up to just about
anyone who asks you

and sometimes you have to call and orange an
orange, get your heart out of your coochie and just
move on
Stop dropping signals that you hope he catches
thinking he'll find value in how good your ass is,
when he'll never dig deep enough to discover the real
treasure that goes so far beyond the moments of
physical pleasure
Questioning why he won't ever choose to stay around
when I made the agreement that I'd always be down,
but for what who knows cause as far as this goes,
there's no need to weigh the pros and cons like a
debater when I know I'm still gonna let him hit it-
later

9/29/15

Author's Note...

I really appreciate each and every one of you who have thought enough of me to purchase and read my words, as everything I write gives you an intimate glimpse into my personal life and things that move and impact me. I hope at the least that I've inspired hope and imparted something worthwhile to your daily processes to help you cope with life and get from it all you want and deserve. This book is a prelude to my 1st spoken word album which will include the pieces in this book performed, as well as bonus tracks. Please follow me on Facebook at https://www.facebook.com/Queen-Cadeena-the-Quintessence-437663053242943 (Queen Cadeena the Quintessence), for updates on books, albums, and live performances. I'm also available for bookings, more information, and feedback by email at cdeparker00@hotmail.com. My sincerest thanks and appreciation for your support!

-Christina D Parker,

Queen Cadeena the Quintessence